WORKBOOK

for

GOOD INSIDE

A Guide to Becoming the Parent You Want to Be

June Willison

This Book Belongs To

_____

_____

_____

Disclaimer

This workbook is an unofficial companion to the original book. It is not endorsed, sponsored, or associated with the original author or publisher of the original book. All views and opinions expressed in this workbook are those of the author and do not necessarily reflect those of the author or publisher of the original book.

Introduction

Throw away the sticker charts and fall in love with your children again.

Some people have tried sticker charts and time-outs and then gave up. You're not the only one. Parents all over the world are joining support groups and buying help books to try to change the bad behavior of their children.

But maybe standard methods of discipline and charts shouldn't be the center of parenting. This Book is proof of that.

In her book Good Inside, Dr. Becky Kennedy talks about getting rid of parenting styles that don't work and changing how you interact with your children.

You can use connection-based methods and set limits while teaching your child how to deal with their emotions and experiences without fear, shame, or self-doubt. It's all in this book.

You won't stop temper fits.

You won't stop fights between siblings or emotional breakdowns.

But you will build strong, long-lasting bonds with your kids that will give them the tools they need to grow up to be strong, confident people. Plus, you won't have to deal with parental guilt, hopelessness, or fear anymore.

Now let's get to parenting.

Chapter 1

Behavior is not the problem

Let's get one thing straight: your child is good on the inside. Not a thing. He feels good when he hits his little sister with a shoe. She's happy inside even when she tells you she hates you.

What's going to happen next starts with agreeing with the "good inside" idea. Since everyone is good on the inside, you'll start to see their actions in a more positive light when you treat your kids, yourself, and everyone else with this mindset.

When things get tough, the first thing you should do is take a deep breath and pick the MGI (most generous reading) of what's going on. Using the MGI helps you talk to your child with kindness and a desire to learn, instead of getting angry and blaming them.

The next thing you need to do is accept that two things can be true at the same time. Sometimes the two things don't get along with each other. For example, you don't let your child have ice cream for breakfast, even though they want to. If you let both of those things be true, you won't feel like you have to change how your child feels.

This means that the good inside method isn't about respecting kids' feelings and giving them whatever they want. Instead, it's about respecting their feelings and setting limits.

You need to know your job, which is the last piece of the puzzle you need to build better interactions with your kids. You should know that it's your job to set limits, not to change how your child feels.

Let's learn how to add to these ideas now.

Key Lessons

- Your child is inherently good inside, even when they behave badly. This shift in perspective is crucial for approaching challenging situations with compassion and understanding rather than frustration and blame.

- Choose the most generous interpretation of your child's behavior. Instead of jumping to conclusions, take a breath and consider the most positive explanation for their actions. This fosters connection and encourages open communication.

- Embrace the dual truth. Accept that your child's feelings and your boundaries can coexist without negating either. You can acknowledge their emotions while still holding firm to your established rules.

- Honoring feelings doesn't mean giving in. Respecting your child's emotions doesn't require giving them everything they desire. You can validate their feelings and uphold important boundaries simultaneously.

- Your job is to set boundaries, not change feelings. As a parent, it's your responsibility to guide your child and establish clear expectations. However, their emotional response is beyond your control. Focus on guiding their behavior without trying to manipulate their feelings.

Practical Exercise

Choose a recent challenging situation with your child.

Write down the situation and identify 3-5 possible interpretations of their behavior.

Situations	Behaviours (MGI)

Choose the most generous interpretation (MGI) and write down how it affects your perspective and response.

_____

_____

_____

_____

Reflect on how approaching the situation with the MGI might have been different from your initial reaction.

_____

_____

_____

_____

Reflection Questions

Do you truly believe your child is inherently good inside, even when they misbehave? If not, what hinders your belief, and how can you work to cultivate it?

_____

_____

_____

How does this belief affect your emotional response to your child's challenging behaviors?

_____

_____

_____

How might it shift your parenting approach and communication style?

_____

_____

_____

Can you recall a recent instance where you jumped to conclusions about your child's behavior? What was the situation, and what was your initial interpretation?

_____

_____

_____

Now, practice the MGI exercise. What are 3-5 alternative interpretations of their behavior?

_____

_____

_____

How would choosing the MGI have affected your response and the outcome of the situation?

_____

_____

_____

Reflection Notes

_____

_____

_____

_____

_____

_____

_____

_____

Chapter 2

Never too late

Let's talk about a worry that a lot of parents have when they learn this new way to talk to their kids. People worry that it's already too late.

Don't be afraid; it's still not too late. It's never too late. Let's go back to the idea that two things are true. As a parent, how you deal with behavior in the early years is very important, and it's never too late to heal and change how you parent.

The first few years of a child's life are important because their bodies store memories long before they can remember them. People in their lives who make them feel safe and loved are known to them. They bond and connect. Strangely, the safer they feel with a parent, the more they are free to be interested, explore, and push the limits.

Your child learns a lot about themselves from how you deal with disagreements when they are young. How you handle your child's behavior that pushes the limits and causes problems shapes their identity.

Of course, if you're past the early years and aren't sure if it's too late, it's not. Neuroplasticity means that the brain can change how it works based on new knowledge. With your child's help, you can change the closing of things that happened in the past that you don't like. This is called repair.

Repair means reconnecting after being disconnected. It means thinking about a fight that went badly, saying sorry, and thinking about what you wish you had done instead. Then you should go up to the child and be ready to understand their point of view. I'll say more about fixing it soon. First, let us talk about why being happy isn't that important.

Key Lessons

- It's never too late to change your parenting: While the early years are important for emotional development, it's never too late to make positive changes in your parenting approach and heal past interactions. Your brain and your child's brain can learn and adapt throughout life.

- The early years matter for building secure attachment: Early responses to your child's needs and emotions establish a foundation of trust and security. This sense of safety encourages them to explore the world and develop their personality.

- How you handle conflict shapes your child's personality: Your responses to your child's challenging behaviors, especially during the early years, teach them valuable lessons about themselves and how to handle conflict in their own lives.

- Repair can rewrite the ending: Even if you have past interactions you regret, you can actively repair the relationship with your child. This involves acknowledging your mistakes, expressing genuine remorse, and seeking to understand your perspective.

- Happiness isn't the ultimate goal: While happiness is desirable, the chapter suggests that focusing on connection, understanding, and emotional intelligence are more important aspects of raising well-adjusted children.

Practical Exercise

Write down a specific parenting situation where you felt frustrated or ineffective.

_____

_____

_____

_____

Now, rewrite the scenario using the "two-things-are-true" approach: acknowledge your past actions while emphasizing your commitment to positive change.

_____

_____

_____

_____

Reflection Questions

What specific worries or questions come up when you think about changing the way you parent?

_____

_____

_____

Can you think of events from the past that might have caused these feelings?

_____

_____

_____

How can you change the way you think about "too late" to give yourself more power and put learning ahead of regret?

_____

_____

_____

Imagine the perfect bond between a parent and a child. In the present, what steps can you take to move toward your goal?

_____

_____

_____

Think back to your own childhood attachment experiences. How do they influence your interactions with your child?

_____

_____

_____

What aspects of your child's behavior resonate with the "boundary-pushing" and "conflict-heavy" descriptions?

_____

_____

_____

Reflection Notes

Chapter 3

Resilience Over Happiness

Being happy isn't the main goal.

If you want to be happy, bad thoughts will get in the way. And everyone should be able to feel what they want. If you want to be a good parent, you should never try to change, judge, or avoid your child's feelings.

You do want your kids to be happy. But staying out of fights, not believing in your own emotions, and thinking you're "bad" for not being happy can all cause worry in the future. Resilience is a much better goal to work on. A child who is resilient can control their behaviors, understand and trust their feelings, and be happy with the way they look.

Being resilient isn't about getting what you want. Remember that your job is to set limits, not to manage how your child feels. It's okay to just sit through the temper fit sometimes.

You need skills like understanding, listening, acceptance, and presence to teach resilience. You need to be able to teach your kid how to solve problems on their own and figure out what they're good at. Being kind and loving to yourself is just as important as being kind and loving to your child.

So, teaching kids to think in terms of connections is also a way to improve yourself. We can only have good relationships with other people, even our kids, if we have good relationships with ourselves first.

Being resilient means working on both yourself and your child's behavior. Behavior shows you what they are thinking and feeling. When strange things happen, remember to give the behavior the benefit of the doubt, tell yourself two truths, and approach it with a desire to understand.

Let's talk about how to change how you act now.

Key Lessons

Shifting focus:

- From happiness to resilience: Instead of pursuing happiness as the ultimate goal, focus on fostering resilience in yourself and your child. This involves managing emotions, understanding them, and feeling comfortable with who you are.
- From controlling feelings to accepting them: Accept and validate all feelings, both positive and negative. Avoiding or judging certain emotions can lead to anxiety down the line.

Building resilience:

- Holding boundaries, not controlling emotions: As a parent, your role is to guide and set boundaries, not control your child's feelings. Allow them to experience and express their emotions freely, even if they're negative.
- Developing key capabilities: Cultivate empathy, active listening, acceptance, and presence in yourself to effectively guide your child through challenging emotions.
- Teaching problem-solving: Help your child identify their strengths and learn to solve problems independently, building confidence and resilience.

Connection and self-reflection:

- Inner work for an outer effect: the relationship you have with yourself is the basis for all other relationships. You can show your child how to treat others by loving and respecting yourself first.
- Relationship-based thinking: Being a parent isn't just about raising your child; it's also a process of personal growth. Prioritizing your own health is necessary if you want to build safe and caring relationships with your child.

How to deal with bad behavior:

- Generous interpretation: When someone acts in a way that you don't expect, look for the good reason behind it. Think to yourself, "What could my child be trying to say?"
- The idea of "two truths": Note that different points of view can exist at the same time. Most of the time, there is more than one right answer. Both sides may have good points.
- Understand what you're doing: Instead of judging or getting angry, try to understand how your child feels and what they need. This makes it safe for people to talk and find an answer.

Practical Exercise

Take 5 minutes every morning or evening to list 3 things you're grateful for. This can be anything big or small, from a delicious meal to a kind interaction. Focus on feeling the appreciation rather than just thinking about it.

_____

_____

_____

_____

Write down your feelings throughout the day, without judgment.
Notice patterns and triggers for negative emotions

_____

_____

_____

_____

_____

_____

_____

Reflection Questions

Reflect on a time you chased happiness as a goal. How did it feel? Did it lead to lasting satisfaction?

_____

_____

_____

What does resilience look like for you? How can you shift your parenting goals to prioritize it?

_____

_____

_____

How do you typically react to your own negative emotions? How can you practice acceptance and validation instead?

_____

_____

_____

What are your biggest fears about letting go of control over your child's emotions? How can you practice trust and acceptance instead?

_____

_____

_____

How can you deepen your understanding of your own emotions and your child's? What resources or practices could help?

_____

_____

_____

Think of a past conflict you faced with your child. How could you have approached it differently to encourage their problem-solving skills?

_____

_____

_____

Reflection Notes

Chapter 4

You First

We've already said that the only thing that will make your relationships with other people better is the relationship you have with yourself. If you're like most parents, you've felt ashamed at some point. It's important to accept your shame, call it what it is, and talk about it. You are doing this to heal yourself and to be able to spot shame reactions in your kids and help them deal with those tough feelings.

Kids get frozen by shame. They are stuck in a tough spot. Let's say your son lies and says he hit his sister with his shoe. No, it's not because he's a rude little liar. He can't decide if he wants to feel bad about hitting his sister or worry that he'll lose the love and safety he needs from you.

You can get him out of it by understanding how he feels about being ashamed, helping him tell the truth, and letting him know that his safety and mental well-being are not in danger if he makes a mistake.

Sharing is the best way to get over shame. Kids can feel safe enough to make the right choice on their own. Don't forget that your child is good on the inside. It is possible to make a setting that helps them be good on the outside as well. Telling the truth is one way to connect with others and feel safe. Kids may have questions during times of high stress. Tell them the truth in easy-to-understand ways so they can understand their feelings and the world around them better.

Remember that you deserve the same kind of treatment as your kids as you start to treat them with kindness and honesty. When you take care of yourself, you give yourself what you need to look good. Take a deep breath, let your feelings out, meet your needs, understand that other people might not like what you want, and heal any damage you've caused to yourself.

We've already said that a relationship is the best way to deal with shame. We're going to talk about how to build relationship capital with your kids next.

Key Lessons

- Start by dealing with your shame. How you treat yourself affects how you treat other people. Recognize and deal with your shame so it doesn't get in the way of your relationships with your kids.

- Know that children feel shame. When kids act out, it's usually because they feel ashamed or afraid of losing love and safety. Understand how they feel and help them get through these tough emotions.

- Connection is very important. Shame grows when people are alone, but a connection can help fight it. Kids should feel safe and secure in their surroundings so they can be open and honest.

- Be honest and open with your kids. Tell them the truth in a way they can understand. This helps them trust each other and understand the world around them.

- Take care of yourself: Put your health first. Make sure you take care of your mind and body so you can be the best parent you can be for your kids.

Practical Exercise

Reflect on situations where you feel ashamed as a parent. Explore the triggers and underlying beliefs behind your shame.

Situations	Triggers / Beliefs

Reflection Questions

What were your expectations for yourself or your child in that situation?

_____

_____

_____

How did those expectations clash with reality? What underlying beliefs about parenting or your own capabilities were challenged?

_____

_____

_____

Did societal expectations, family dynamics, or comparisons to other parents contribute to your shame?

_____

_____

_____

How did these external factors influence your internal narrative?

_____

_____

_____

Reflect on past experiences, particularly your own childhood, that might have shaped your sensitivity to certain triggers. How do those past experiences color your present parenting reactions?

_____

_____

_____

What core values do you hold dear as a parent? Did your actions in that situation align with those values? If not, what internal conflict arose?

_____

_____

_____

Reflection Notes

_____

_____

_____

_____

_____

_____

_____

_____

_____

Chapter 5

Connection is Key

It takes time to build relationships. This isn't something that can be fixed and left alone. It is important to make, keep, and grow connections.

One way to do that is to set aside time to talk to them without their phone. Turning off your computers and the internet for a week is not necessary. Just make sure that your kids see you put down your phone and pay attention to them on a regular basis.

A way to connect with kids before big events is through emotional vaccines. You and your child might talk about what will happen before the first day of school. Take note of any worries or other emotions you have. Please tell a story about a similar thing that happened to you.

The problem is not how you feel. The trouble is feeling alone in your feelings. A child's "feeling bench" is a metaphor for how they feel when something big is going on that they don't understand.

It's sometimes enough to just sit with them on the bench and let them know you're there for them.

Repairing things is probably the most important way to build connections, and we've already talked about it. Your goal should never be to keep relationships from ending, because that's not possible. You'll make your relationships stronger and teach your kids the skills they'll need to be strong in the future if you learn how to fix things.

To fix things, you need to think about what went wrong, admit it, say what you would do better, and then connect with curiosity and understanding.

Building relationships is an ongoing process that makes the best setting for kids to bring their best selves to the outside world. However, it doesn't stop bad behavior. In the next part, we'll talk about bad behaviors first, and then good behaviors that look bad.

Key Lessons

- Connection takes work: If you want to have strong connections with your kids, you have to keep working at it. It's not a one-time fix; you have to keep working on building, maintaining, and expanding your relationship.

- Give your child an emotional shot: talk to them about how they're feeling before a big event or change, and share your own similar experiences. You'll feel closer to them because they'll know you understand and are ready.

- Give your child a safe place to talk about their feelings. Your child can use a "feeling bench" or another metaphor for a safe spot where they can say what they're feeling without being judged. It can be very comfortable to just sit with them and let them know they're not alone.

- Learn how to fix things. Breakups in relationships are unavoidable, but knowing how to fix them well can make your bond stronger.

- In order to fix something, you need to think about what happened, admit your part in it, say what you would do differently, and then connect with curiosity and understanding.

- Connection leads to good behavior: Making strong links sets the stage for good behavior, but it doesn't completely stop bad behavior.

Reflection Questions

What are your biggest fears about building strong connections with your children? How can you address these fears and move forward?

_____

_____

_____

How do you currently prioritize focused time with your children? What changes could you make to be more present and engaged?

_____

_____

_____

Think back to a time you felt truly connected with your child. What were the circumstances?

_____

_____

_____

What can you learn from this experience to replicate in the future?

—————————————————————————————————

—————————————————————————————————

—————————————————————————————————

Have you ever practiced emotional vaccination with your children? How did it impact your relationship? Share a specific example.

—————————————————————————————————

—————————————————————————————————

—————————————————————————————————

What does the concept of a "feeling bench" evoke for you? How could you create a safe space for your child to express their emotions without judgment?

—————————————————————————————————

—————————————————————————————————

—————————————————————————————————

Reflection Notes

_____

_____

_____

_____

_____

_____

_____

_____

Chapter 6
When Disconnection Occurs

Good kids sometimes act badly. Most of the time, bad behavior is caused by fear, a lack of connection, or unmet wants. The most likely reason your child isn't listening to you is that you're not connecting with them. It doesn't matter how loud you talk; they won't hear you. Wait until you can connect with them again after a break before telling them what you want them to do.

When a child's mental needs are too great, it can show in their body. When a kid can't handle their feelings, they may have emotional or aggressive tantrums, as well as feelings of fear and anxiety.

As a mom, you want to make sure your kids are safe first. Your job includes taking the child away or holding them down if you need to. Keep the lines clear. Inform your kid that they can't hit their sister. Your child will know they can count on you when you say "I won't let you." They should know that you'll keep them and other people safe.

After making sure your child is safe, talk to them. Find out why they lost control and help them understand. Remember to be honest.

Problems with attachment can also lead to bad actions, such as fighting with siblings or lying. When this happens, a child probably worries that they will lose touch with you or their place in the world. Get to know your child, understand them, and tell them the truth. Remember that the goal is not to get them to stop doing it, but to give them the confidence to do so on their own.

Feeling helpless can make you rude, defiant, and whiny. These habits are hard to deal with because they usually make you mad or upset. Before you go up to your child, you should think about why the behavior bothers you. Get in touch with your kid and talk about your job and their work. Help them figure out how much power they can safely have while still following the rules you set and trusting that you will give them room to grow.

These are a few of the most common things people do when they feel disconnected or their needs aren't met. Our next set of actions has a different cause.

Key Lessons

- Misbehavior as a Signal: Bad behavior in children isn't just about defiance; it often indicates a deeper issue like lack of connection, unmet needs, or fear.

- Connection over Correction: When children misbehave, yelling or punishment is ineffective. Instead, focus on re-establishing a connection before addressing the behavior.

- High Emotional Demands: Tantrums and anxiety might indicate emotional overload. Help children regulate their emotions through calm connection and understanding.

- Safety First: Ensure physical safety first. Set clear boundaries and restrain if necessary but with reassurance and love.

- Truth and Empathy: After ensuring safety, connect with your child, empathize, and honestly explain why their behavior was unacceptable.

- Attachment and Fear: Sibling rivalry or lying can stem from attachment issues. Reassure your child of your love and help them feel secure.

- Powerlessness and Control: Rudeness, defiance, and whining might be cries for control. Connect with your child, discuss your roles, and help them find safe ways to exercise control within boundaries.

- Remember: The goal isn't just to stop the behavior, but to create a safe environment for your child to learn and regulate themselves.

Reflection Questions

Have you ever shut down and punished your child after misbehavior, only to realize later it stemmed from a deeper issue? What did you learn from that experience?

_____

_____

_____

How can you become more attuned to your child's emotional needs and signals, even when they haven't expressed them verbally?

_____

_____

_____

Think of a time you truly connected with your child on a deep level. What was happening? How did it affect your relationship?

_____

_____

_____

What sets you off when you feel too much emotion? How can you manage your emotions to better help your child?

_____

_____

_____

How can you give your child a safe place to talk about their feelings, even the bad ones, without fear of being judged?

_____

_____

_____

Think about a time when you helped your child calm down after a bad mood. How did you go about it? What learned did you get out of it?

_____

_____

_____

Reflection Notes

_____

_____

_____

_____

_____

_____

_____

_____

Chapter 7

Understanding What's Normal

A lot of parents worry about habits that are perfectly normal. Behaviors like shyness, intolerance of anger, food problems, tears, and striving for perfection are all signs that a child needs to take charge of their surroundings.

That's a good sign when you see a child hesitant to join the group. They want to know what's going on before they join in. Your child will be better off if you talk to them about something important ahead of time or if you sit with them while they're unsure and answer any questions they may have. You shouldn't force them into something they don't want to do. If you push them into doing something they don't want to do, you will tell them their feelings are wrong. That will stop them from being able to trust their feelings.

Controlling the surroundings is also a part of not being able to handle frustration, crying, and trying to be perfect. You shouldn't try to get your child over these feelings. Instead, you should help them keep moving through them. It's good for kids to be able to keep working even when they're angry or upset.

Share stories from your own life with your child and make them feel safe being in their feelings.

A lot of the time, parents start fights over food. A parent's most basic duty is to feed their child. It's hard to deal with when your child doesn't like the food you're giving them. Always keep in mind that it's your job to feed them well. You're not supposed to make them eat it.

In the end, you want your child to be strong and sure of themselves as an adult. You want them to be able to handle tough situations, know what consent means, set their own limits, and see their relationships grow. Not believing in themselves will make them lack confidence. You have to show them how to trust their feelings by being with them when they're feeling good, setting limits, and helping them see the good in themselves.

Key Lessons

- Understand that seemingly challenging behaviors are often a child's way of trying to control their environment. This includes shyness, frustration intolerance, food challenges, tears, and perfectionism. These are normal behaviors and a sign of healthy development.

- Support your child's exploration rather than pushing them into situations they're not comfortable with. When a child hesitates, acknowledge their feelings and help them understand the situation before jumping in. Don't force them or dismiss their feelings.

- Focus on helping your child navigate difficult emotions, not eliminating them. Allow them to feel frustrated, cry, or strive for perfection while providing support and guidance. Share your own experiences and help them feel safe expressing their emotions.

- Remember that food battles are often driven by parental anxieties. Your job is to offer healthy food, not force them to eat it. Avoid making mealtimes a power struggle and focus on creating a positive and relaxed environment.

- The ultimate goal is to raise confident and resilient children who trust their own feelings. By modeling trust, holding boundaries, and helping them recognize their strengths, you can equip them to navigate challenging situations and build healthy relationships.

Reflection Questions

Reflect on your own childhood: Can you recall instances where you exhibited shyness, frustration intolerance, food challenges, tears, or perfectionism?

_____

_____

_____

How did your own parents (or caregivers) respond? Did their approach help or hinder your emotional development?

_____

_____

_____

Think about a current or past child in your life who displays seemingly challenging behaviors. What are the triggers for these behaviors?

_____

_____

_____

How could you, as a parent or caregiver, respond differently to support their exploration and understanding of their emotions?

_____

_____

_____

What are your hopes and dreams for your children? Do these expectations sometimes lead to frustration or pressure when children's behaviors don't conform?

_____

_____

_____

How can you reframe your expectations to be more aligned with healthy emotional development?

_____

_____

_____

Conclusion

The good-inside method to raising kids is all about love and respect in the end. Most of the things that kids do should be easy to understand. We still do a lot of those things as adults, after all. Know that behavior isn't the issue and that improving behavior isn't the main goal. Your kid is good on the inside. They're acting that way for a reason. You need to connect with them before you can change how they act. It's your job to set rules. And when you do these things, you make your child feel safe, loved, and good about themselves.

Reflection Notes

_____

_____

_____

_____

_____

_____

_____

_____

Reflection Notes

_____

_____

_____

_____

_____

_____

_____

_____

Reflection Notes

Reflection Notes

_____

_____

_____

_____

_____

_____

_____

_____

Reflection Notes

Made in the USA
Coppell, TX
20 June 2024

33718636R00037